EDWARD ELGAR

FIVE PIANO IMPROVISATIONS
TRANSCRIBED BY IAIN FARRINGTON

NOVELLO

COVER DESIGN Fresh Lemon Ltd

Order No. NOV121242
ISBN 1-84609-604-9

© 2006 Novello & Company Limited

Published in Great Britain by Novello Publishing Limited
Part of the Music Sales Group

HEAD OFFICE
14/15 Berners Street
London W1T 3LJ
England
Tel +44 (0)20 7612 7447
Fax +44 (0)20 7612 7549

SALES AND HIRE
Music Sales Distribution Centre,
Newmarket Road,
Bury St Edmunds,
Suffolk IP33 3YB,
England
Tel +44 (0)1284 702600
Fax +44 (0)1284 768301

www.chesternovello.com
email: promotion@musicsales.co.uk

All Rights Reserved

Printed in Great Britain

No part of this publication may be copied or reproduced in any form or by
any means without the prior permission of Novello Publishing Limited.

PREFACE

Although apparently professing a dislike for the instrument, Elgar used the piano extensively when composing, and would expand and elaborate his ideas through improvisation at the keyboard. The most notable instance of this was the genesis of the *Enigma Variations*, when Elgar improvised several of the variations in one evening to his wife Alice. He was no virtuoso; he played in an idiosyncratic, orchestral manner, quite unlike 'acceptable' pianism, but nonetheless effective enough for the thorough exploration of new ideas.

More than any of his contemporaries, Elgar embraced the new possibilities in recorded sound, and from 1914 he enthusiastically conducted many of his own works for record. The nineteen-twenties saw very little compositional activity from Elgar and it may be that the recorded piano improvisations were an attempt to use the recording process to stimulate progress on new work. In a recording session in the Small Queen's Hall, London, on 6th November 1929, Elgar improvised five pieces at the piano, each around 4½ minutes in length (restricted by the typical length of one side of a 78 r.p.m. record). These recordings lay unheard for many years, until their first release in 1975; they offer fascinating insights into Elgar's working process and pianism.

Elgar opens his first improvisation with a melody from the ballet in the first act of Rossini's *William Tell*. While remaining faithful to the melody, he drastically slows the original tempo, and 're-orchestrates' with rich harmony in spread chords. After an extemporised opening, the second improvisation incorporates a noble melody derived from *Fate's Discourtesy*, a song from Elgar's 1917 wartime Kipling setting, *The Fringes of the Fleet*. Perhaps Elgar's subsequent disillusionment with that era and its empty optimism is felt with the sombre minor key ending. The most technically demanding and brilliant improvisation is the third. Out of the opening four chords, Elgar presents a scurrying theme, with busily weaving chromatic scales. This is repeated in numerous keys and registers with ease, suggesting the material was well known to Elgar. Similarly, the bulk of the fourth improvisation was probably well established in advance, as Elgar wrote this out as the slow movement for his never-completed Piano Concerto. It is Elgar's lighter-music vein at its very best, with an attractive lilting quality.[1] The fifth improvisation is the most profound of the set, with wistful falling melodies and tender harmonies. It is unclear how much of the material is completely improvised, but the piece is by far the most poignant and nostalgic of the five. Its closing A♭ major melody is possibly a distant echo of the opening of the First Symphony, written over twenty years earlier.

In transcribing these improvisations I needed to strike a balance between an 'accurate', detailed transcription and an accessible score from which to play. Several difficulties were encountered when transcribing the works. The poor sound quality of the recordings, along with Elgar's extensive use of the pedal, often made the pinpointing of exact detail difficult. Both in terms of rhythm and tempo, Elgar's playing is exceptionally free, causing uncertainty over a precise rhythmic layout, and his exuberant performance contains some obvious inaccuracies. The improvisations do not bear the structural perfection of Elgar's written works, and the question arose of whether to adjust the material to build more rigorous forms.

A score that attempted to document exactly all of Elgar's figurations, pedalling and rubato would be confusing and dogmatic. Thus, my priority in notation was to create a clear text that is akin to any other Elgar work. In order to overcome the difficulties presented by the recording and to obtain the most accurate representation of Elgar's performance, I listened to the improvisations many times, notating the music at the piano as I heard it, and playing simultaneously with the recording once it was written down. Despite the lack of clarity and Elgar's occasional inaccuracies, the harmonic and melodic outlines of each piece could be easily established, as Elgar repeats much of his thematic material. These repetitions allowed an 'ideal' version of each theme to be notated and used for analogous places in each piece. For example, the principal theme of the third improvisation is rarely played in a 'correct' manner, as Elgar prefers to blur the sound and smudge the detail. Rather than attempting to reproduce Elgar's more approximate rendering, I decided to notate precise chromatic scales for each appearance of the theme, in keeping with the rondo structure and Elgar's style.

Where Elgar uses inner arpeggios to 'fill in' the sound, I have notated these in a precise but straightforward manner. Rhythms with the potential for written complexity, I tidied to an extent, while retaining some of the capriciousness of the original to avoid stiffness. An example of this approach can be found in bar 4 of the first improvisation, where Elgar consistently appears to play the theme in the following manner:

After some consideration, I decided to retain Rossini's original rhythm, taking the rhythmic distortion to be Elgar's unique use of rubato. To highlight this rhythmic elasticity, there is a judicious use of tenuto markings and tempo indications throughout the score. The slight subtleties of rubato are not specified, leaving the performer free to produce an individual interpretation. Metronome marks give a basic tempo guide, but these rarely hold for more than a bar's length as Elgar's tempos constantly fluctuate.

Elgar used the pedal generously, clothing the sound in warmth and resonance. Given that every piano demands an individual approach, and Elgar's pedalling is often erratic, I have not notated his pedal changes, allowing the performer complete flexibility. Although often self-evident, more pedal is better than less, and Elgar's recording is the ideal guide.

Finally, rather than making any 'improvements' to the work, I have retained Elgar's own harmonic and structural solutions, true to the improvisatory nature of the original. Obvious blemishes have been deliberately polished, all within the Elgarian style, without sacrificing the occasional moment of harmonic spice. The inaccuracies and ambiguities are extensive, and to annotate each would lead to an over-complex score with abundant footnotes. Thus, the score is my own realisation of Elgar's performance, acting as the basis for a much freer reading than the fixed notation might suggest. With the luxury of foresight that the completed score offers, it is possible to give different interpretations of Elgar's improvisations, perhaps highlighting neglected themes or varying the pace of the overall structures.

Elgar composed only around a dozen works for piano, mostly miniatures (except the substantial Concert Allegro), and these five transcribed improvisations are therefore a considerable addition to this slender repertoire. They can be performed as a group, individually or in different combinations, and are easy to programme in any piano recital. While the performer is certainly urged to investigate the original recordings, and what they might reveal through repeated hearings, it is hoped that these transcriptions will inspire pianists to find their own solutions in interpreting and recreating Elgar's improvisations.

Iain Farrington © 2005

---

[1] Robert Walker's realisation of the Elgar Piano Concerto places the movement in a broad symphonic context, making much use of the third improvisation.

FURTHER LISTENING

Elgar's recorded improvisations are available on EMI 7243 5 85153 2 9.

Robert Walker's realisation of the Elgar Piano Concerto is available from Dutton Laboratories (CDLX 7148), performed by David Owen Norris (piano) and the BBC Concert Orchestra conducted by David Lloyd-Jones.

David Owen Norris has also recorded the Elgar improvisations, playing by ear rather than set notation. This is available on Elgar Editions EECD002.

FIVE PIANO IMPROVISATIONS

1.

EDWARD ELGAR
transcribed by
IAIN FARRINGTON

© 2006 Novello & Company Limited

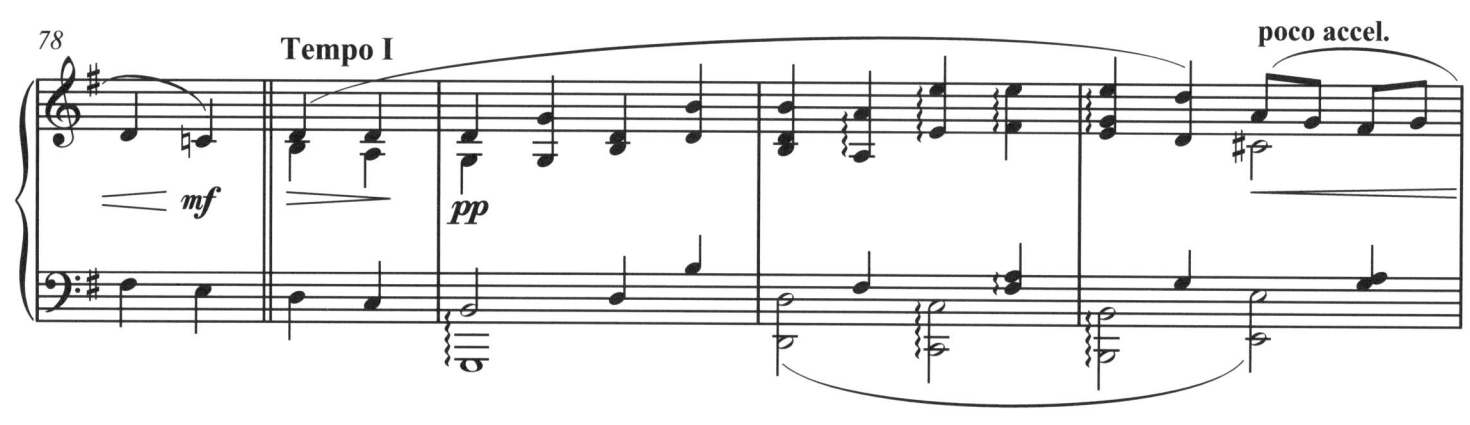
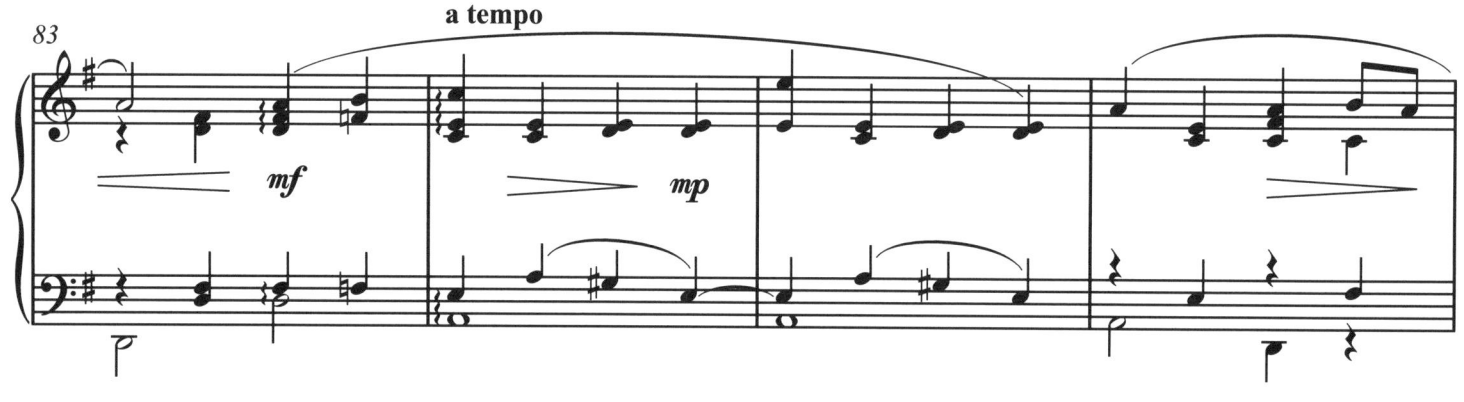
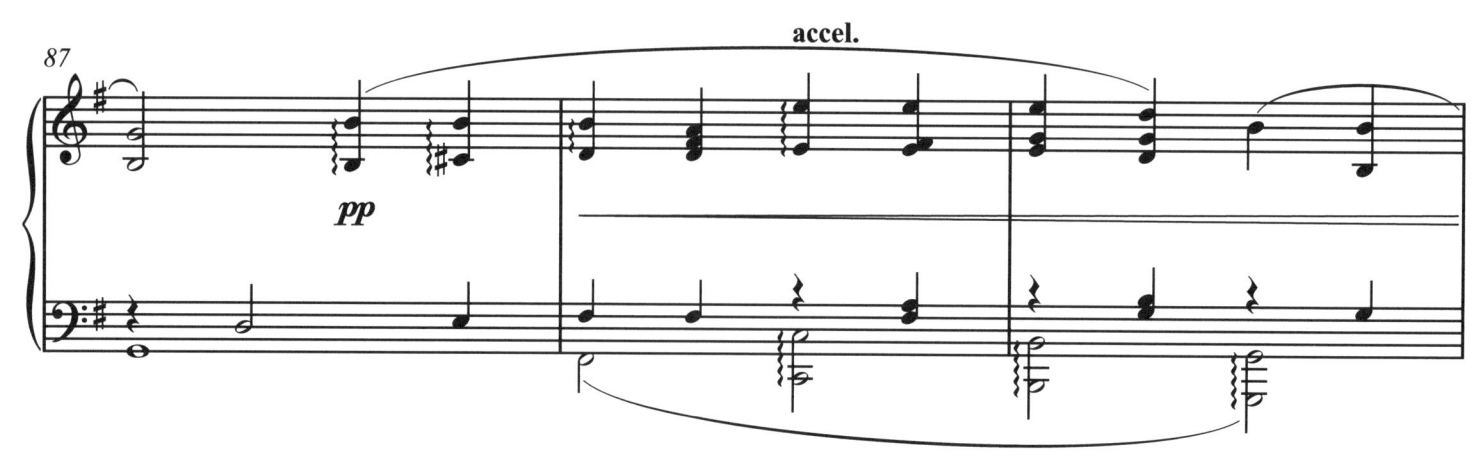

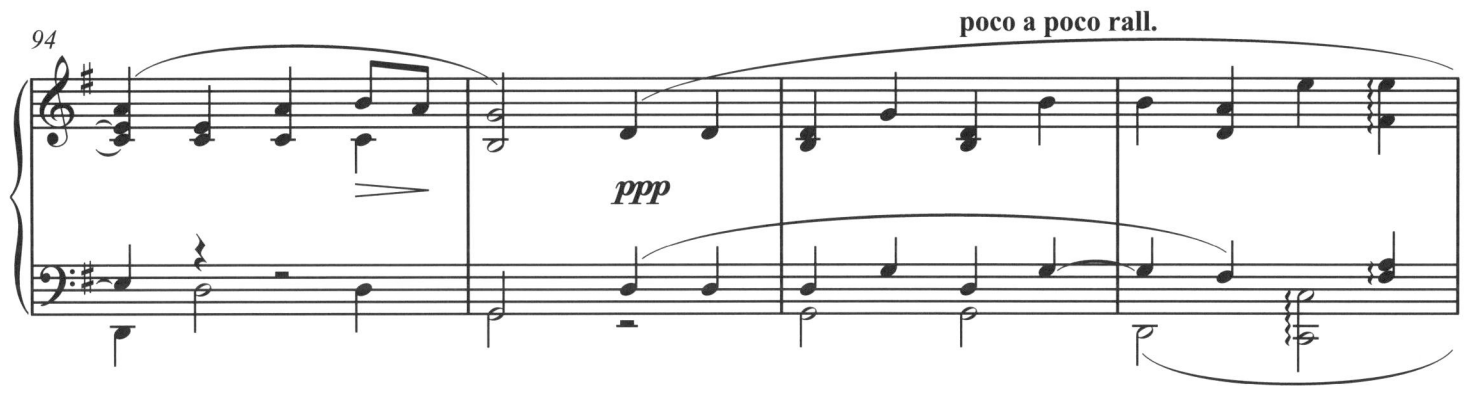

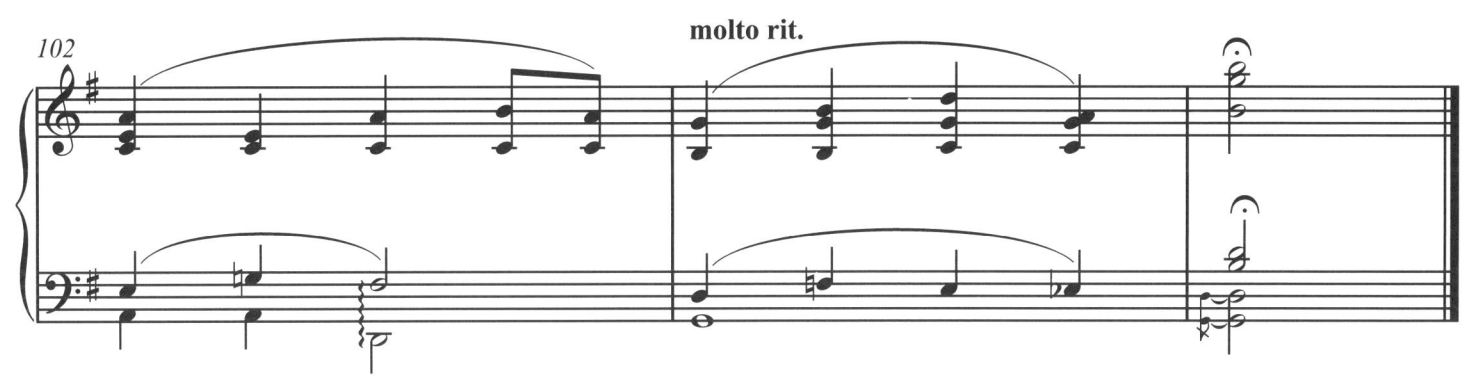

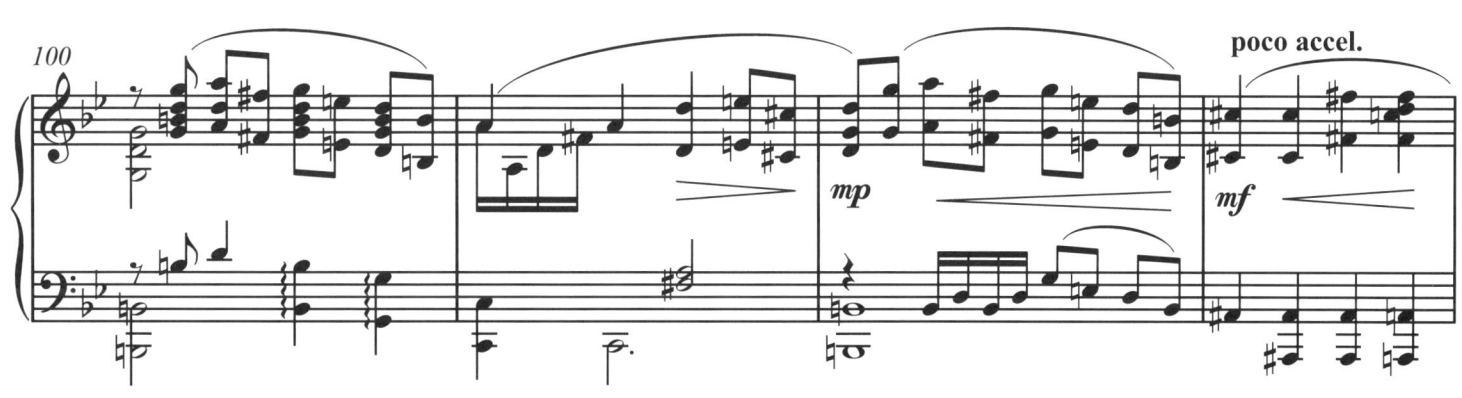

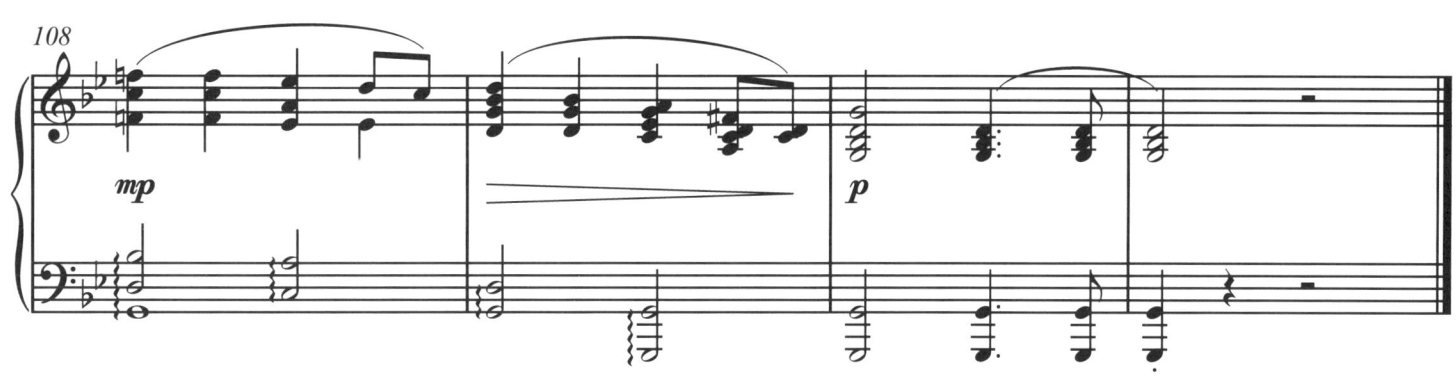

3.

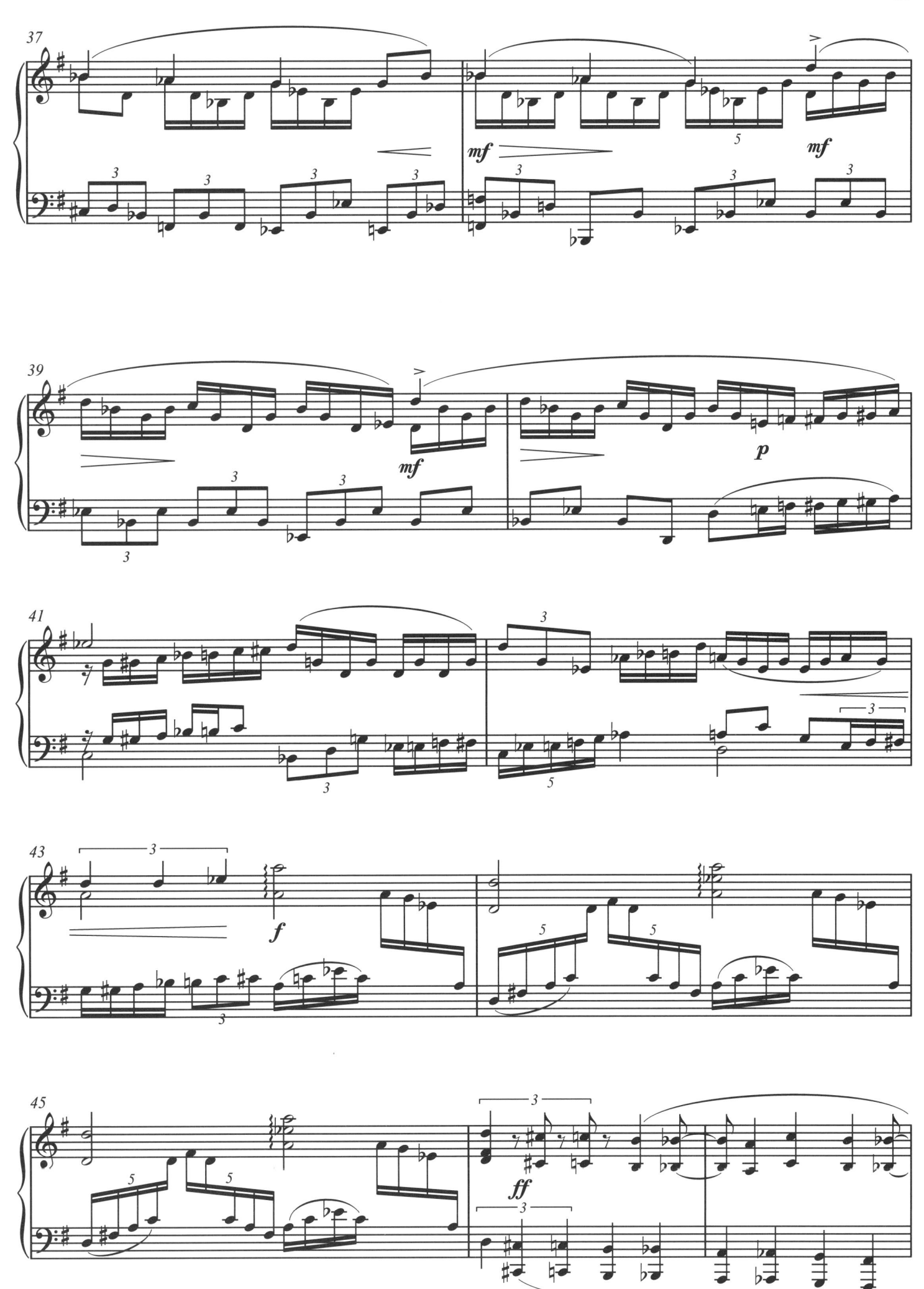

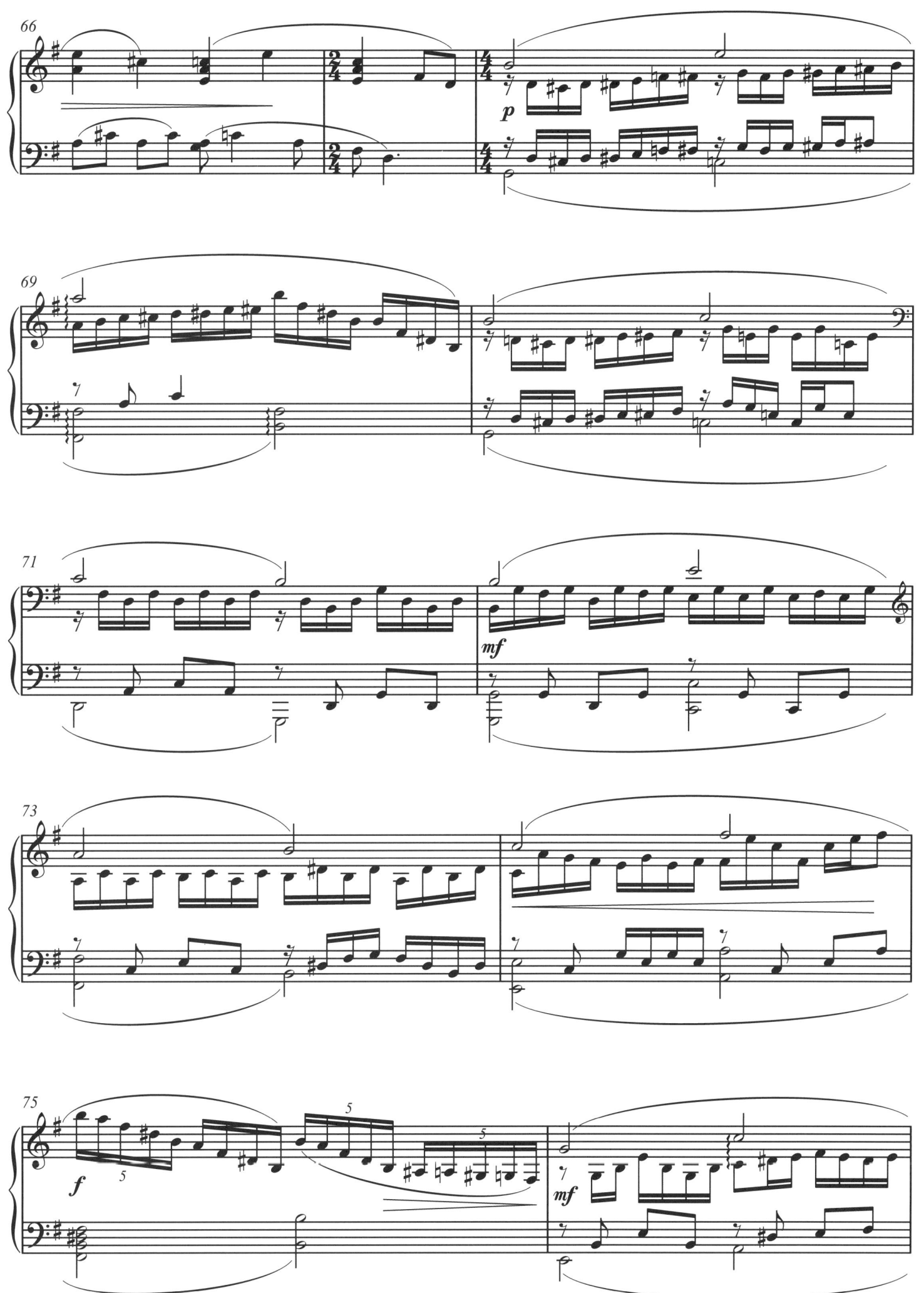

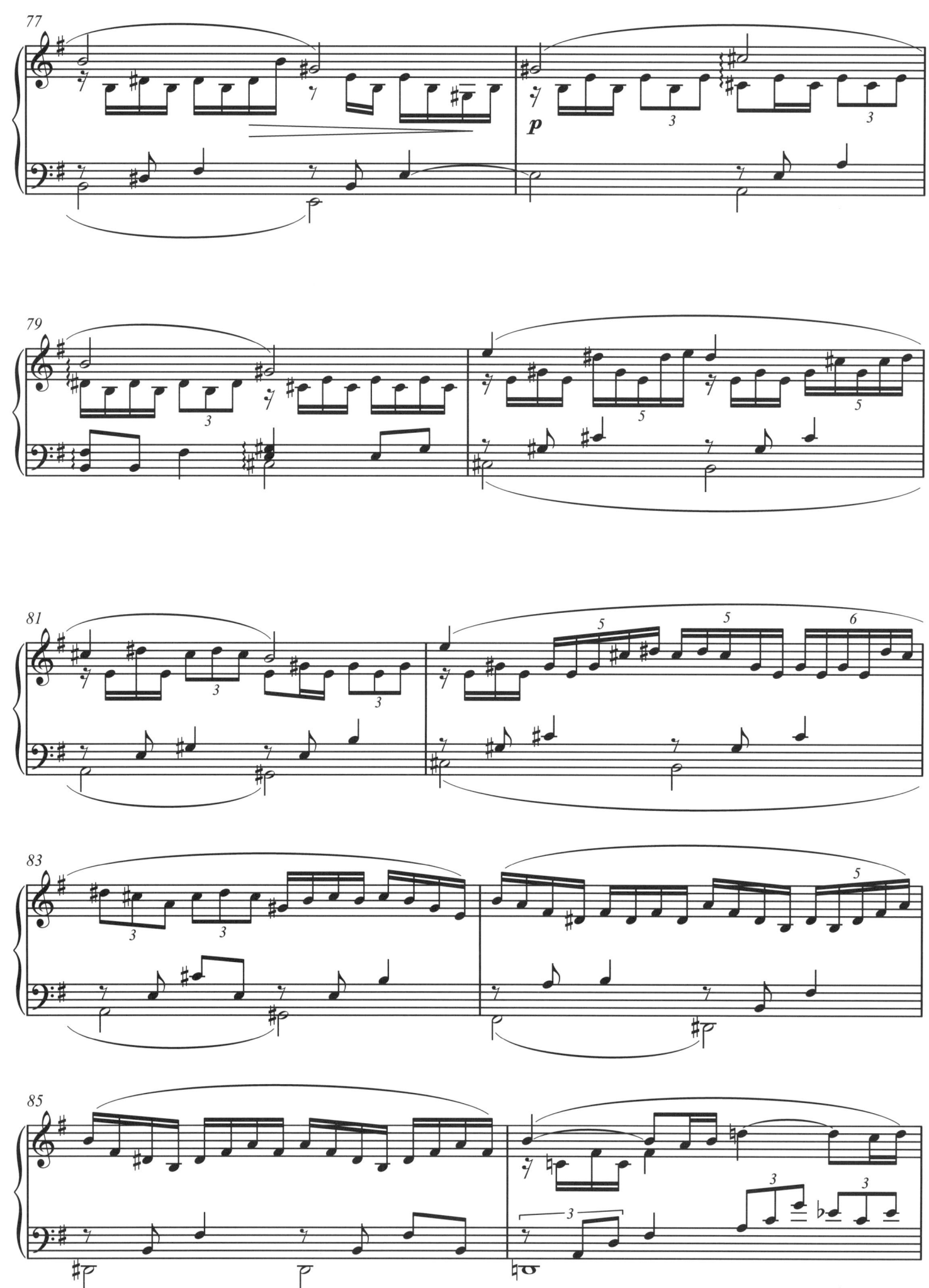

4.

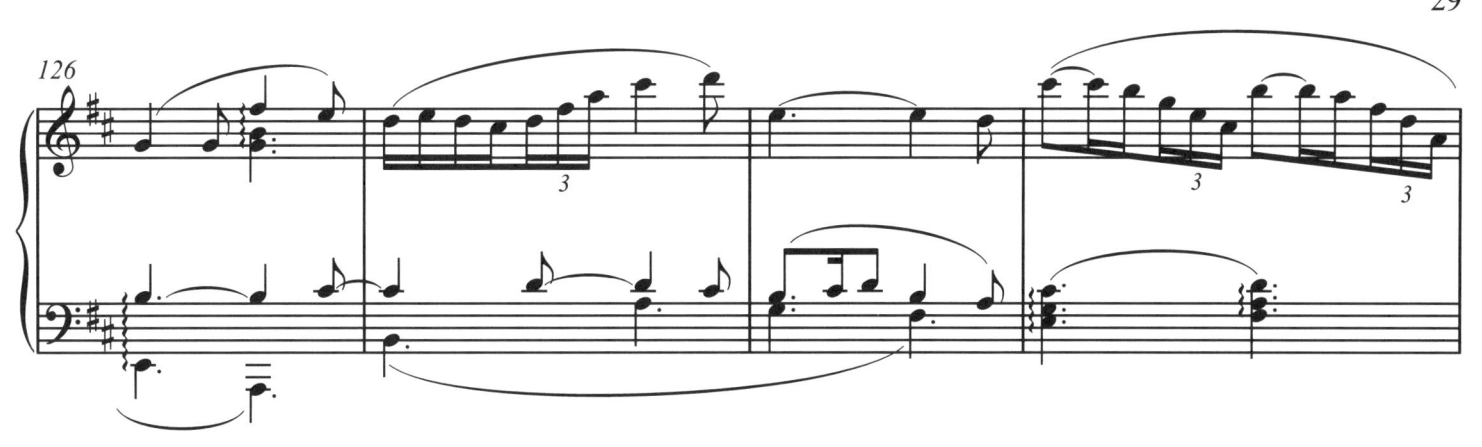
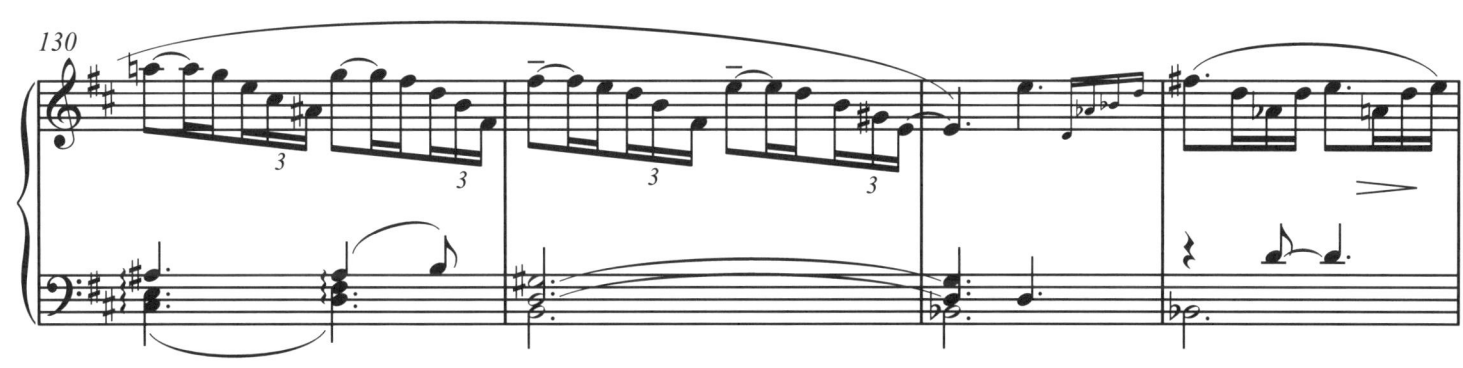

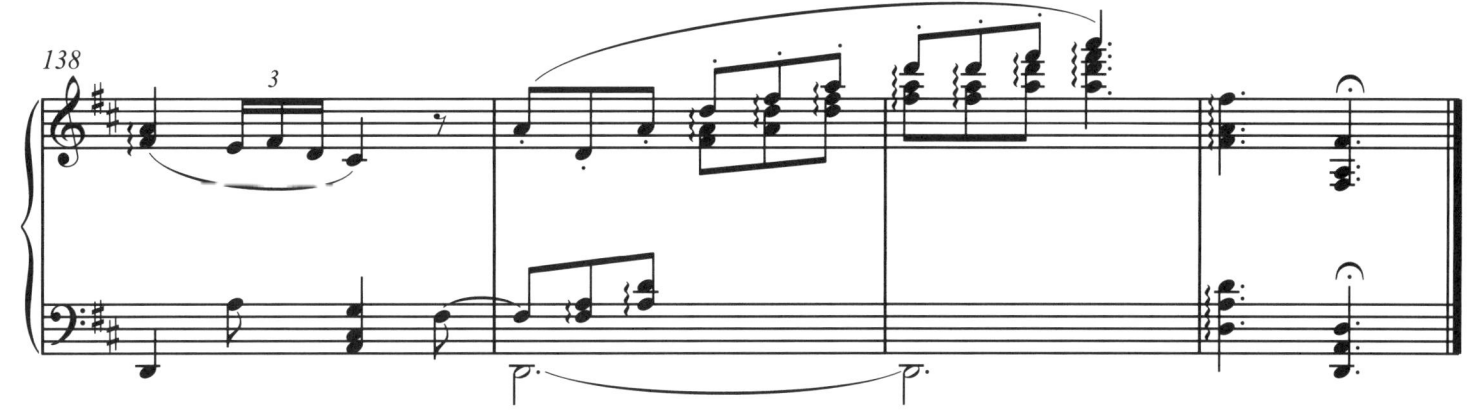

5.

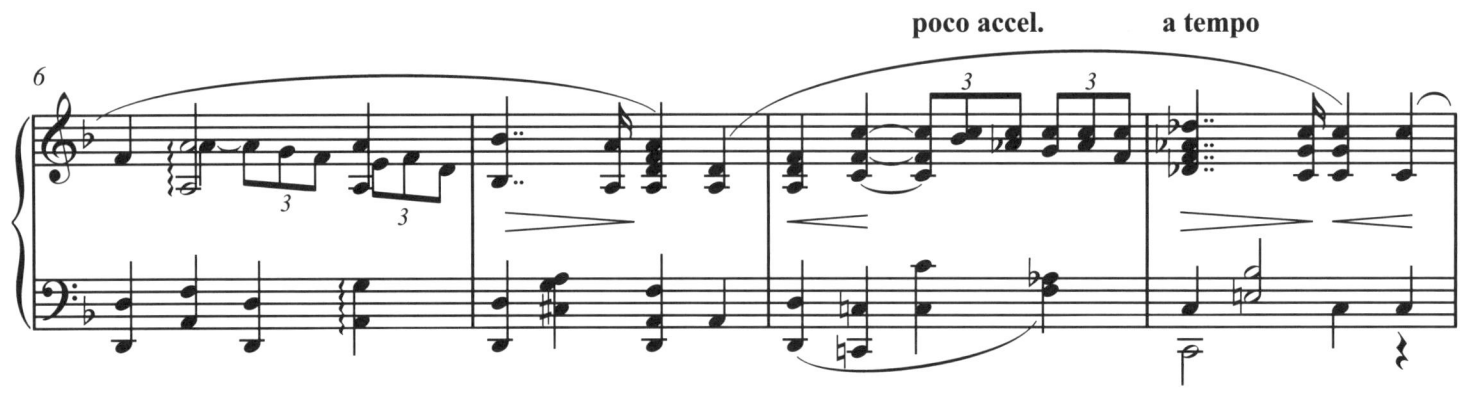

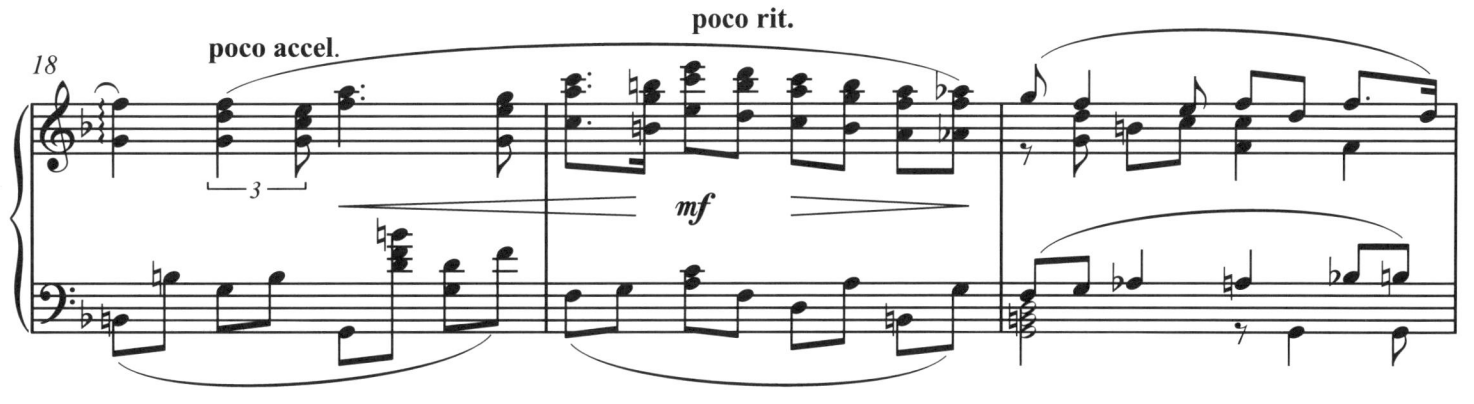
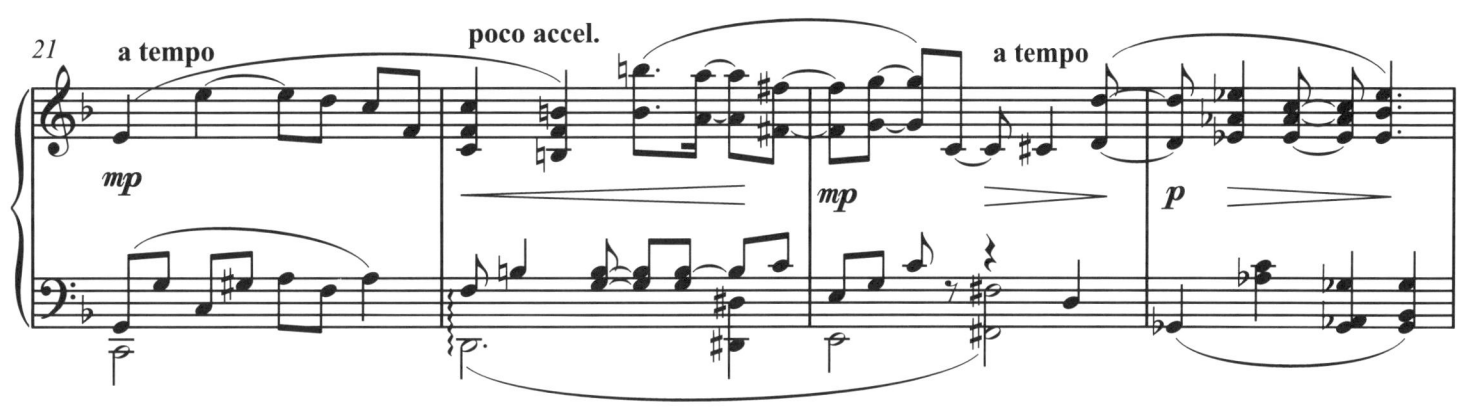
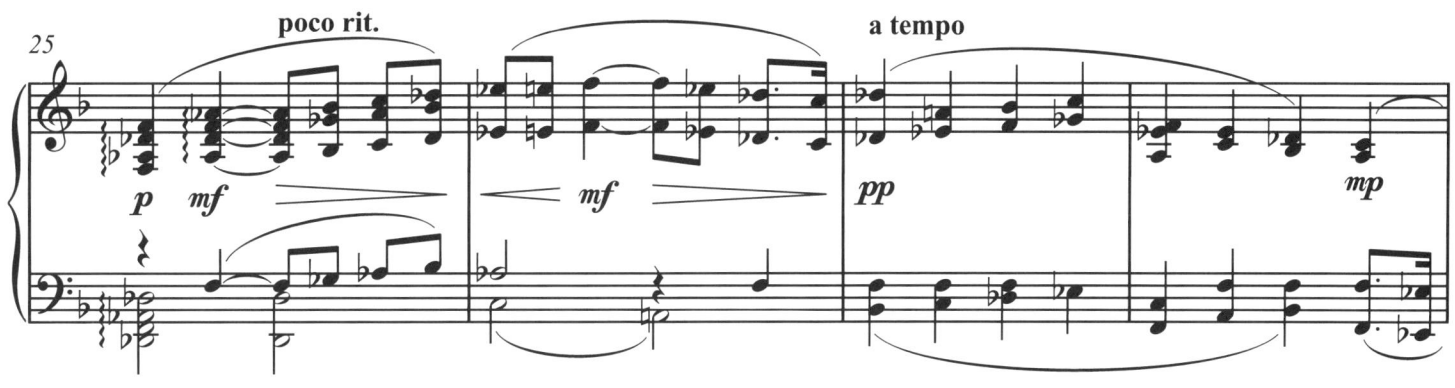